A PASSION FOR ELEPHANTS

The REAL LIFE ADVENTURE of Field Scientist Cynthia Moss

by **Toni Buzzeo**   illustrated by **Holly Berry**

Dial Books for Young Readers

an imprint of Penguin Group (USA) LLC

DIAL BOOKS FOR YOUNG READERS
Published by the Penguin Group
Penguin Group (USA) LLC
375 Hudson Street
New York, New York 10014

USA * Canada * UK * Ireland * Australia
New Zealand * India * South Africa * China
penguin.com
A Penguin Random House Company

Library of Congress Cataloging-in-Publication Data
Buzzeo, Toni.
A passion for elephants: the real life adventure of field scientist Cynthia Moss / by Toni Buzzeo ;
illustrated by Holly Berry.   pages cm
ISBN 978-0-399-18725-4 (hardcover : acid-free paper)
1. Moss, Cynthia—Juvenile literature. 2. African elephant—Kenya—Amboseli National Park—Juvenile literature. 3. Amboseli National Park (Kenya)—Juvenile literature. I. Berry, Holly, illustrator. II. Title.
QL737.P98B89 2015   599.67'4—dc23   2013025476

Manufactured in China on acid-free paper

1 3 5 7 9 10 8 6 4 2

Designed by Mina Chung · Text set in Lomba
The art was created using colored pencils, acrylic paint, watercolor, ink, and collage on rag paper.

To Cynthia Moss and all the dedicated elephant
advocates of Amboseli Trust for Elephants

— T.B.

Dedicated to the Matriarchs: those strong leaders who
nurture, protect, and teach future generations how to
survive and get along in life

— H.B.

Imagine a horse with a back so high
you can't even see over it.
Now imagine a little girl, just seven years old,
riding atop that great, tall horse,
so high up, so far from the hard ground.
That little girl was Cynthia Jane Moss.
She was not afraid.
Cynthia Moss was not afraid of **BIG** things.

By the time Cynthia was twelve,
she galloped on her very own horse, Kelly,
near her home in Ossining, New York.
She and Kelly found deer and foxes
that made her love the woods in which she rode—
and all of nature—even more.

At sixteen, Cynthia set out on her
first solo adventure away from home.
She traveled more than four hundred miles south
to attend a school in far-off Virginia
where everyone loved horseback riding
just as much as she did.

Later, when Cynthia graduated from college,
she didn't know that soon
she would begin her grandest adventure—
and become a scientist too!

While Cynthia was working as a magazine reporter,
Penny, a college friend, wrote her letters from Africa,
the second-largest continent on Earth.
When Cynthia read Penny's letters,
she longed to go see Africa for herself.
Many people might be afraid to go off to Africa all alone.
But Cynthia Moss was not afraid of that **BIG** continent.

When Cynthia arrived, she fell in love with Africa.
"Within a week of getting there," she said,
"I had this overwhelming sense that I'd come home."
Cynthia wanted to spend her life
on the wide-open savannahs of East Africa.

But she needed a job.

Luckily, Cynthia met a zoologist studying African elephants.

He invited Cynthia to photograph those elephants,
the most **ENORMOUS** land animals on planet Earth.

Imagine that you have a camera
and a park full of huge elephants
with their tiny brown eyes,
their wrinkled gray hides,
their long, strong, flexible trunks,
and their soft padded feet.
At first they all look alike.

But Cynthia studied the veins and notches, holes and slits,
on the outer edges of the elephants' ears.
She looked for their long ivory tusks—
curved, straight, broken, or even missing.
She learned to tell the elephants apart.

Before long, Cynthia fell in love
with those **ENORMOUS**, gentle animals,
just as she loved their wild and dusty home.
"They were such impressive,
remarkable, and complex creatures," she said,
"that I wanted to devote my life to studying them."
So she started the Amboseli Elephant Research Project.

Cynthia didn't know that she had found her life's work.
She only knew that she wanted to learn more.
More about how elephants live in families
—and groups larger than families—
when the rains are long and grasses
are lush.
More about how they help each
other to survive
when the rains are short and
days are parched.

Just as before, she began by taking photographs.
Cynthia said, "I would take the photographs home
and pore over them using a magnifying glass . . .
and try to sort out all of the ears."
She also gave them human names,
using the same initial letter for members of one family:
Adam, Agatha, Albert, Alyce, Amy, Annabelle,
and . . . Wart Ear,
because sometimes, she couldn't help keeping
the very first name that came to her mind.

Finally, she began to learn
who were the mothers and fathers,
who were the sisters and brothers,
who were the aunties and grandmothers.
It was a **BIG** job,
but Cynthia Moss was not afraid of **BIG** things.

Meanwhile, Cynthia built a permanent camp
in Amboseli National Park.
Her thatched-roof tent had a view
of the snow-capped peak of Mount Kilimanjaro,
the highest mountain in Africa.

Cynthia drove her Land Rover out into the park each day
to see baby elephants with floppy trunks
squirming and scrambling in the mud.
She saw mother elephants standing guard
against hungry lions and spotted hyenas.
And when separated elephants found each other again,
she saw them spin their bodies, wrap their trunks together,
flap their ears, and click their ivory tusks,
all while trumpeting, rumbling, and screaming hello.

Cynthia also saw the grandmothers, or matriarchs,
who remembered the best places for food and water
even in years when no rain fell.
She watched and learned from her special favorite, Echo,
the beautiful grandmother with long curving tusks.
Imagine a time later, when that beautiful matriarch
walked slowly toward Cynthia's Land Rover
and stopped close enough to almost touch her,
saying hello with her quiet gaze.

As she watched, Cynthia learned what no one else knew
about elephant family behavior.
"Elephants do the kinds of things we'd like our best
friends to do," Cynthia said.
"They defend each other, they take care of each other,
and they cooperate with each other."

But not all humans loved elephants as much as Cynthia.
In just ten years' time, half of Africa's elephants were killed.
During those years, at least one elephant in the world
died every ten minutes.
Imagine watching a huge male elephant
strolling through the savannah,
uprooting grasses and small bushes with his curving tusks
and munching them quietly under a vast sky.
Now imagine that the very next day
he is lying lifeless in the beating sun,
his beautiful ivory tusks missing,
used to make piano keys, carvings, or jewelry.

As the oldest male and female elephants
with the longest, most valuable tusks disappeared,
Cynthia worried about elephant families.
Who would become the father elephants?
Who would protect the baby elephants?
Who would show the families where to find food and water?

Cynthia began to speak out about ivory.
She said that ivory is a beautiful substance
that glows like nothing else when it is carved.
But, she said, people forget
that ivory is the tooth of a living elephant,
and that greedy poachers kill that elephant for its tooth.
She joined others in the fight
to make selling ivory illegal all over the world.
It was a **BIG** challenge,
but Cynthia Moss wasn't afraid of **BIG** things.

NO IVORY EVER

STOP the IVORY TRADE

SAVE the Elephants

SAY NO TO IVORY

In January 1990, a global ban was passed on the sale of ivory.
But not all countries agreed with the ban,
and so the ivory fight has not ended.
Many people still want ivory so badly,
they will kill a gentle African giant for a tooth.
Cynthia continues to speak out against it.

More than forty years of days and nights
have passed on the African savannah
since Cynthia Moss started the Amboseli Elephant Research Project.
Cynthia, that horse-loving little girl, couldn't have dreamed
that the Amboseli elephant families would be her life.
She has studied more than two thousand five hundred elephants.
She has watched their births and their deaths,
even the death of her beloved Echo in 2009.

Although she is often away now,
giving lectures, raising money,
Cynthia has never stopped studying the elephants
and sharing their stories around the world,
in speeches, in films, in books for children and adults.
She has given her life
to the longest study of wild elephants ever undertaken,
to learning everything she can about Echo, Echo's children,
and all of the elephants of Amboseli still to come.

It is an **ENORMOUS** job.
But Cynthia Moss is not afraid of **BIG** things.

CYNTHIA MOSS was born in 1940 and has spent the past forty years living with and studying the elephants in Amboseli National Park in Kenya.

After graduating from Southern Seminary in Virginia, she went on to Smith College and studied philosophy. Two years after graduating from college in 1962, Cynthia landed a job working at *Newsweek* magazine as a reporter and researcher. Had it not been for the long, descriptive letters she received from her college friend Penny Naylor in Africa, she might never have gone to see the continent for herself in 1967. She might never have fallen in love with both the place and, ultimately, the elephants. Because both of her parents had passed away, she had few family ties, except for her older sister, Carolyn, to hold her in the United States, and so she moved to Africa.

When Cynthia was first in Africa, she was lucky to meet Scottish zoologist Iain Douglas-Hamilton, who was studying elephant social interactions in Lake Manyara National Park in northern Tanzania. In order to recognize individual elephants, he needed photographs of all four hundred in the park. He hired Cynthia to undertake that task. When it was complete, Cynthia longed to start her own research project, which she was finally able to do in September 1972 with fellow researcher Harvey Croze. Together, they established the Amboseli Elephant Research Project in Amboseli National Park, which is 150 square miles of protected land in southern Kenya. When Croze left in 1974, Cynthia stayed on and has remained with the elephants ever since.

Cynthia's passion for learning more about the elephants has never waned. She has been patient and faithful in her study of them. As a result, she has learned so much more than she might have if her time with them were briefer or more sporadic. She continues to search for new answers to questions about family relationships among elephants. She speaks about her elephants with great affection, whether she is being interviewed at her campsite in Amboseli or speaking at fundraisers across the world. The elephants are truly her life, as they have been for over four decades.

Other researchers have also been active in studying African elephants. One of the world's greatest authorities is the man who first introduced Cynthia Moss to African elephants, Dr. Iain Douglas-Hamilton. His main research interest is in understanding elephant choices by studying their movements. He helped to bring about the world ivory trade ban in 1989 and founded Save the Elephants (www.savetheelephants.org) in 1993 to ensure a future for African elephants through research, protection, education, and communication.

Another important African elephant researcher, Dr. Joyce Poole, began her work in Amboseli studying under Cynthia Moss, her early mentor. She has now studied the social behavior and communication of African elephants for over thirty years. In 2011, she and her husband, Peter Granli, founded ElephantVoices (www.elephantvoices.org), an elephant conservation project in the Maasai Mara in East Africa.

Africa's elephants are now in critical danger. The more these researchers and others learn about them and share that knowledge, the more likely the people of the world are to work to save the gentle giants Cynthia Moss loves so much.

Photo © IFAW/D. Willetts

FURTHER READING

"Cynthia's Elephants," by Deborah Churchman and Martyn Colbeck. *Ranger Rick*, September
   1994: 18–27.

Hillstrom, Kevin and Laurie, eds. *Biography Today: Profiles of People of Interest to Young
   Readers. World Leader Series: Environmental Leaders 2. Volume 3*. Detroit: Omnigraphics,
   2000. pp. 93–105.

Moss, Cynthia. *Echo of the Elephants: The Story of an Elephant Family*. New York: William
   Morrow, 1993.

Moss, Cynthia. *Little Big Ears: The Story of Ely*. New York: Simon & Schuster, 1996.

Pringle, Laurence. *Elephant Woman: Cynthia Moss Explores the World of Elephants*. New
   York: Atheneum, 1997.

ADDITIONAL SOURCES

Amboseli Trust for Elephants. http://elephanttrust.org/

Brookshire, Isaiah. "Walking with Giants," *Santa Ynez Valley Journal*, June 3, 2010
   http://www.syvjournal.com/article.php?a=6498

Echo, An Elephant to Remember [DVD]. PBS, 2010.

Echo of the Elephants [DVD]. Thirteen/WNET, 1994.

Echo of the Elephants: The Next Generation [DVD]. Thirteen/WNET, 1994.

Moss, Cynthia. *Elephant Memories: Thirteen Years in the Life of an Elephant Family* (With a
   New Afterword). Chicago: University of Chicago Press, 2000.

Robinson, Simon. "Free as the Wind Blows." *Time*, 155:8 (February 28, 2000), 68+
   http://www.time.com/time/magazine/article/0,9171,996234,00.html

Schick, Elizabeth A. "Cynthia Moss: The Elephant Lady," *World & I*, 9:1 (January 1994), 208+